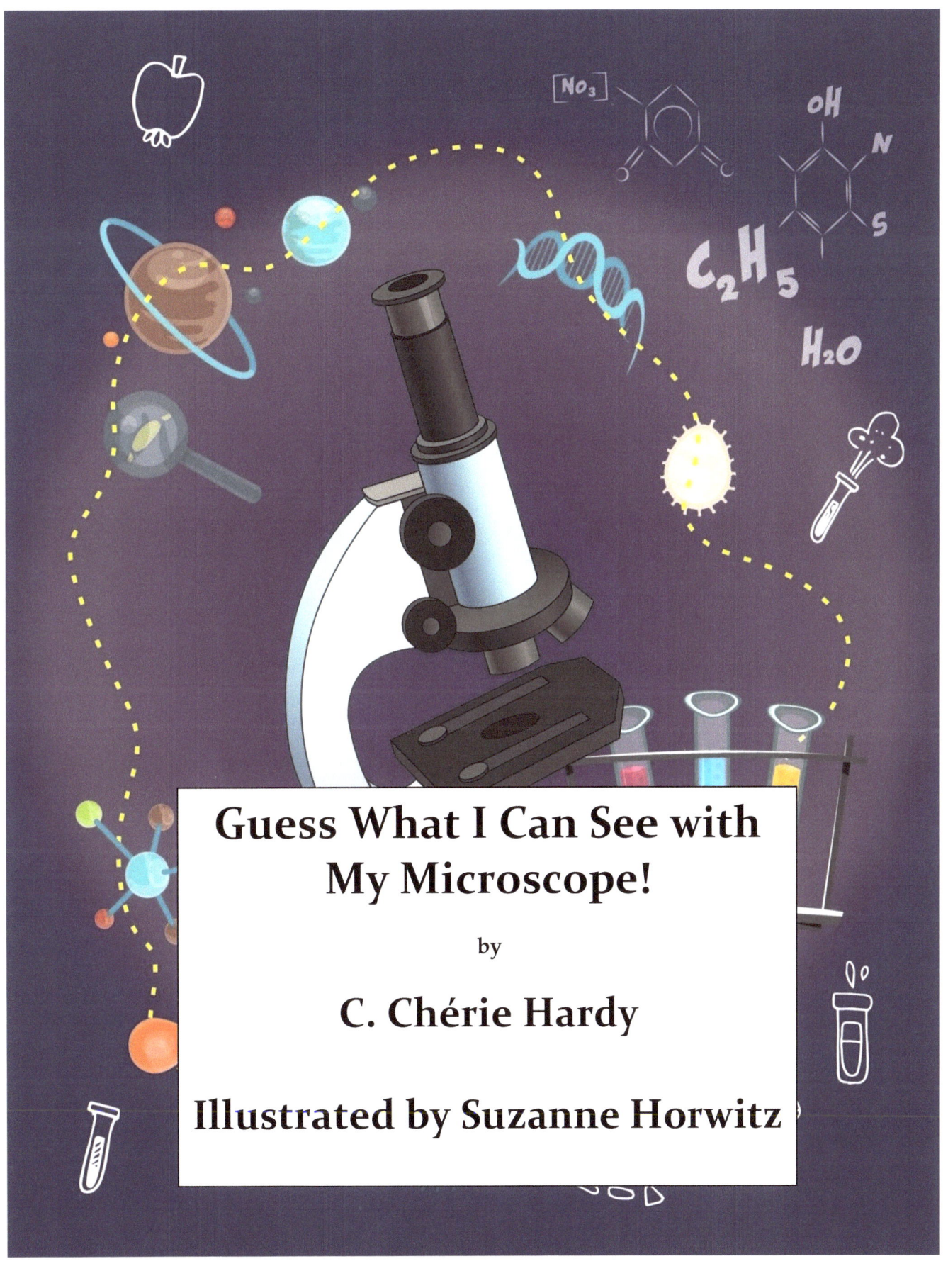

Avant-garde Books
Children's Corner
Post Office Box 566
Mableton, Georgia 30126
www.avantgardebooks.net

Guess What I Can See with My Microscope!

Copyright © 2018 by Corendis Chérie Hardy
All rights reserved.

No part of this book can be reproduced in whole or in part, or stored in a retrieval system, or transmitted in any form or by any means, without permission of the publisher.

Illustrations and cover image by Suzanne Horwitz
All rights reserved.

ISBN: 978-1-946753-28-1

Made in the United States of America

This book is dedicated
to my beloved cousin,
Sean Malcolm Hamilton.

Hey! My name is Malcolm! Biology is my favorite subject in school. **Biology** is the study of living **organisms** and how they function. **Anatomy**, **zoology**, and **botany** are three important branches of biology, but there are more.

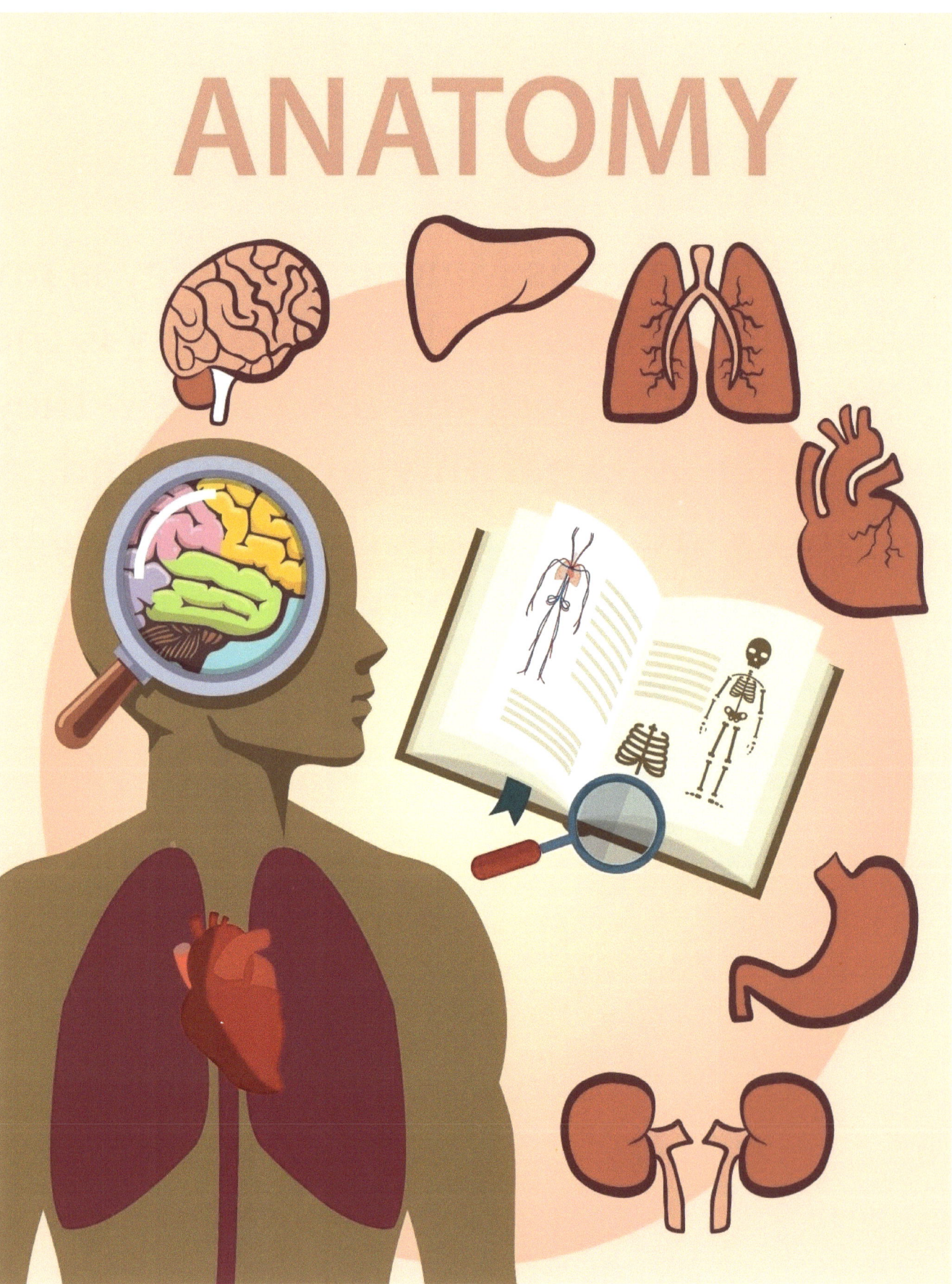

Anatomy is a branch of science that deals with the structure of living things, including human beings. An **anatomist** is a specialist in anatomy.

ZOOLOGY

Zoology is a branch of science that involves the study of animals and animal behavior. **Zoologists** are scientists who study animals.

Botany is a branch of biology that focuses on plant life. **Botanists** are people who study plants. George Washington Carver (1864-1943) was a famous botanist. He discovered over 300 ways to use peanuts. His work was very important to **agriculture** and humanity.

Last year, my grandparents gave me a **microscope** for my birthday. I am so grateful! I love my gift! My microscope allows me to see things that I can't with my naked eyes. It **magnifies** objects that I put under the microscope lens. Living things that are unseen are called **microorganisms** because of their tiny size.

After my dad and I reviewed the instructions for using the microscope, we collected water **samples** from the pond behind our house.

Wow! It was cool seeing tiny **microorganisms** wiggling around. I learned that some are called **amoebas**. They can change their shape and extend themselves. They don't have bones like humans do. And, they can be deadly if they crawl into a person's nose.

Don't tell my mom, but I removed a leaf from one of her favorite plants. I flattened a small piece of the leaf by placing it between two clean microscope slides. It was amazing to see the **intricate** patterns that were not visible to my naked eyes.

Next, I decided to look at the dead spider I found on my windowsill. Using a pair of **tweezers**, I carefully placed the spider on my lens. I was surprised to see that its entire body was covered with tiny strands of what looked like hair. After a little **research,** I found out these hairs are called **trichobothria**. They help spiders hear because they don't have ears like humans do.

I was really amazed about what I saw when I viewed orange juice with my microscope. I would not have guessed I would see such **vibrant** colors!

I was just about to find a new **specimen** when my dad entered my **laboratory**, (which is my bedroom actually) and announced that it was time for dinner. He said I had to put away my **science** stuff but promised I could do more exploring next weekend. Yippee! I really LOVE science!

Here are a few more safe things you can look at with your microscope. Just remember to ask an adult to help you and be careful handling certain items like **bacteria,** insects, and pond water.

bacteria
banana
caffeine
chalk
chocolate cake
Coke cola
dead insects
dirt
dust
fabric
flower petals
fly ash
grass
guitar string
hair
kosher Salt
moss
needle and thread

onion skin
paper
piece of apple
pond water
potato
sand
sea water
snow
soil
spider
strawberries
tears

Glossary

agriculture (noun) – the cultivating of soil, producing of crops, and raising of livestock

amoeba (noun) – a tiny animal that lives in water, and is a single cell that ingests food and moves about (plural: amoebas or amoebae)

anatomist (noun) a specialist in anatomy

anatomy (noun) – a branch of science that deals with the structure of living things, including human beings

bacterium (noun) - a microscopic organism with a single cell that can cause disease (plural: **bacteria**)

biology (noun) – a branch of science that deals with living things and the processes they need to exist

botanist (noun) – a scientist who studies plants

botany (noun) – a branch of biology that focuses on plant life

intricate (adjective) – having many complex interrelating parts

laboratory (noun) – a place where scientists conduct experiments; and engage in scientific research, observations, and analysis

magnify (verb) – to make something appear bigger or greater

microorganism (noun) – a very tiny living thing that can only be seen with a microscope

microscope (noun) – an instrument used for making very tiny things seem bigger

Glossary

organism (noun) – a living thing made up of one or more cells and able to complete functions of life such as growing, using energy, and reproducing

research (noun) – a detailed study about a subject to find and report new information; (verb) – to study a subject (topic); to collect information about a topic

sample (noun) – a small amount of something that gives you information about the object it was taken from

science (noun) – knowledge about the natural world based on the results of experiments and/or observations

specimen (noun) – a small amount or piece of something that can be tested and/or observed

trichobothrium (noun) – a sensory hair on certain organisms such as arthropods other invertebrates (plural: trichobothria)

tweezers (noun) – a small instrument that is used like pinchers for grasping and pulling small things

vibrant (adjective) – very bright and strong

zoologist (noun) – a scientist who studies animals

zoology (noun) – a branch of science that involves the study of animals and animal behavior

Activities

Activity A   (Reading comprehension)

Directions: Complete each sentence with the correct word from the story.

1. Malcolm's _____ gave him a _____ for his birthday.
2. _____ is a branch of science that deals with plant life.
3. The _____ on spiders help them hear because they don't have _____ like humans do.
4. Many lakes and ponds are filled with _____ which are _____ organisms that have no bones.
5. Malcolm and his dad collected water _____ from a pond located _____ their house.
6. Malcolm was able to discover the names of hairs on spiders because he conducted _____.
7. _____ are so small that they cannot be seen with the _____ eyes.
8. A scientist would likely conduct experiments in a _____.
9. A microscope _____ things to make them appear bigger.
10. _____ is Malcolm's favorite subject in school.
11. Zoologists study animals, but _____ study plants.
12. _____ was a famous scientist who discovered over _____ ways to use peanuts.

Activities

Activity B   (Reading Comprehension)
Directions: Answer the following questions.

1. What branch of science deals with plant life?
2. What branch of science focuses on the structures of living organisms?
3. What instrument is used to help people see microscopic organisms?
4. What is the English equivalent for the Greek root, micro-
   (a) big   (b) yellow   (c) tall   (d) very small
5. Where do many scientists conduct experiments?
6. Who was a famous botanist that discovered over 300 uses for peanuts?
7. What do scientists need to test a small amount of something?
8. What instrument can scientists use to grasp small objects?
9. What branch of science deals with the study of animals and animal behavior?
10. What is the study of living things and the processes they need to exist?
11. What microscopic organisms can cause disease?
12. True or False Botanists are specialists in anatomy.

1. _____
2. _____
3. _____
4. _____
5. _____
6. _____
7. _____
8. _____
9. _____
10. _____
11. _____
12. _____

Activities

Activity C **(Science Vocabulary)**
Directions: Find the words specified in the word-search puzzle.

analyze	botanist	microscope	scientist
anatomy	botany	organism	specimen
bacteria	experiment	research	zoologist
biologist	laboratory	sample	zoology
biology	microorganism	science	

```
M U Y D P Y D M H E E L B O B
U S F M N E S F Z Z P E I C I
V E I A O I U O O Y O Y T R O
I S T N N T O Q R L C A Z T L
S O C A A L A O M A S I O P O
B C G I O G T N B N O R O G G
E R I G E A R J A A R E L Q I
O D I E R N H O B I C T O X S
Z S K O N U T C O O I C G K T
T Q B Z I C C I R R M A Y O P
S A M P L E E W S A C B U B M
L N E M I C E P S T E I A Y U
B O T A N I S T U C B S M L A
Z E X P E R I M E N T X E U T
N E R J Y G O L O I B H M R H
```

Activities

Activity D   **(Research)**
Find out more information about the following Black scientists:

Benjamin Banneker (1731-1806)
Patricia Bath (1942)
Guion S. Bluford (1942)
George R. Carruthers (1939)
Benjamin Carson (1951)
George Washington Carver (1864-1943)
Emmett Chappelle (1925)
Marie Maynard Daly (1921-2003)
Cheikh Anta Diop (1923-1986)
Charles Drew (1904-1950)
Philip Emeagwali (1954)
Mae Jemison (1956)
Katherine G. Johnson (1918)
Percy L. Julian (1899-1975)
Ernest Everett Just (1883-1941)
Rick Kittles (1976)
Samuel Massie, Jr. (1919-2005)
Bennet I. Omalu (1968)
Norbert Rillieux (1806-1894)
Neil deGrasse Tyson (1958)
James West (1931)
Daniel Hale Williams (1858-1931)

Answers

Activity A
1. grandparents, microscope
2. Botany
3. trichobothria, ears
4. amoebas or amoebae, microscopic
5. samples, behind
6. research
7. Microorganisms, naked
8. laboratory
9. magnifies
10. Biology
11. botanists
12. George Washington Carver, 300

Activity B
1. botany
2. anatomy
3. microscope
4. (d) very small
5. Laboratory (laboratories)
6. George Washington Carver
7. Sample or specimen
8. Tweezers
9. Zoology
10. Biology
11. Bacteria
12. False

Activity C (next page)

Answers

Activity C

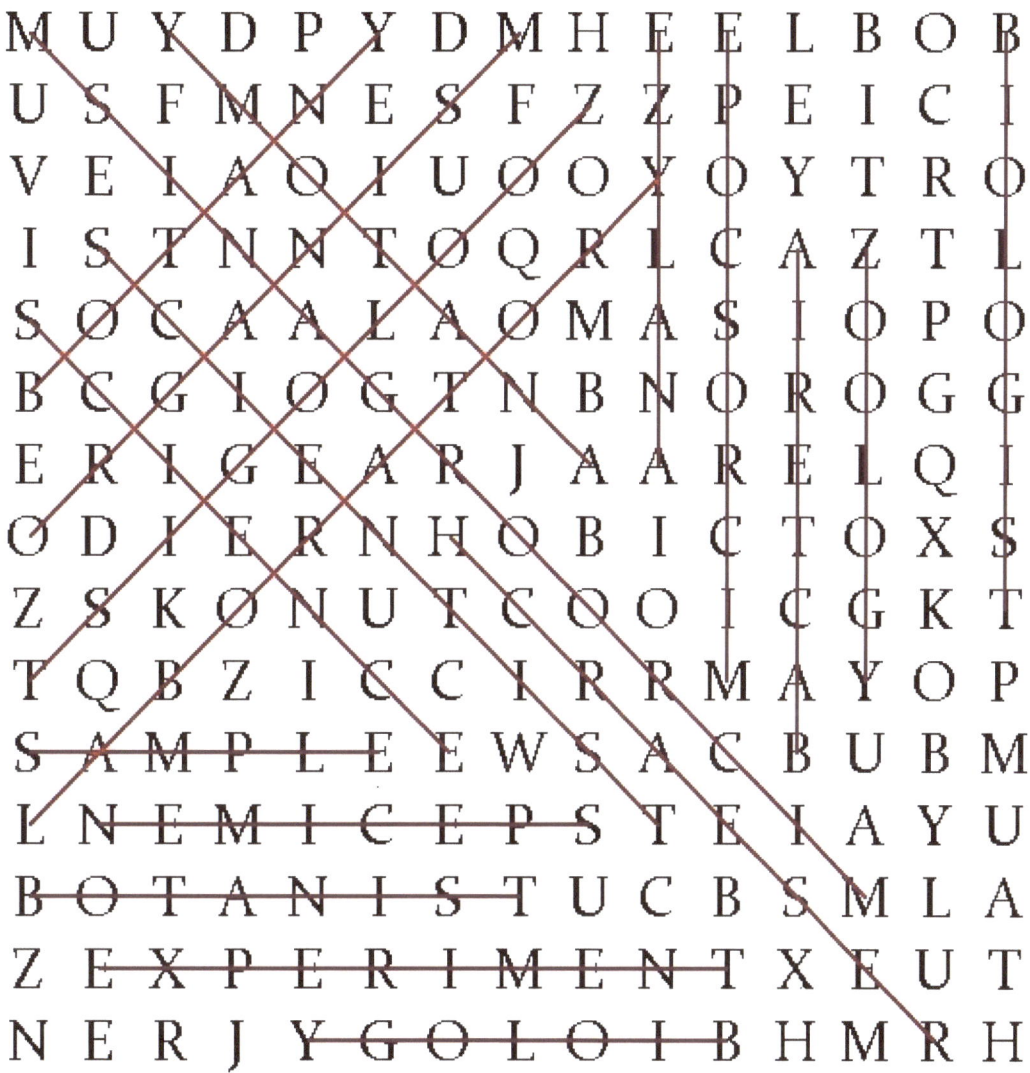

Connect with **Avant-garde Books, LLC!**

Mailing Address:
Post Office Box 566
Mableton, Georgia 30126

Website:
www.avantgardebooks.net

Facebook:
@avantgardebooks100

Twitter:
@Avant_GardeBks

Instagram:
@avantgardebooks

Email:
avantgardebooks@gmail.com

Bibliography

http://animals.mom.me/spiders-hair-bodies-10868.html

https://www.freedrinkingwater.com/resource-guide-to-pond-animals-creatures.htm

https://www.merriam-webster.com/

http://microscopesunlimited.com/how-to-prepare-a-microscope-slide/

http://www.microscopy-uk.org.uk/index.html?http://microscopy-uk.org.uk/pond/

https://sciencing.com/ideas-things-kids-can-microscope-7583120.html

https://study.com/academy/lesson/how-to-use-a-microscope-lesson-for-kids.html

http://www.toptenreviews.com/home/articles/top-10-things-to-see-with-your-first-microscope/

www.ingramcontent.com/pod-product-compliance
Lightning Source LLC
LaVergne TN
LVHW072127070426
835512LV00002B/29